C0-DYE-794

THE EDGE OF THE UNDERWORLD

Michael Ruby

THE EDGE OF THE UNDERWORLD

Michael Ruby

BlazeVOX [books]
Buffalo, NY

THE EDGE OF THE UNDERWORLD
by Michael Ruby

Copyright © 2010

Published by BlazeVOX [books]

All rights reserved. No part of this book may be reproduced without the publisher's written permission, except for brief quotations in reviews.

Printed in the United States of America

Book design by Geoffrey Gatza
Cover photo from Associated Press/The Emporia Gazette/Casey Wilson
© 2001. All rights reserved. Reprinted with permission.

First Edition

ISBN 13: 9781935402831
Library of Congress Control Number: 2009910155

BlazeVOX [books]
Geoffrey Gatza
303 Bedford Ave
Buffalo, NY 14216
Editor@blazevox.org

publisher of weird little books

BlazeVOX [books]

blazevox.org

2 4 6 8 0 9 7 5 3 1

ACKNOWLEDGEMENTS

Poethia: "Sic Fatur Lacrimans," "Sibilance"

Situation: "Verba Sancta"

Nedge: "Avuncular," "Whimsies," "Polymorphous Perverse"

Angle: "Solaces"

Alef Books: "Among Senses," "The Seal Wore Out"

Contents

THE EDGE OF THE UNDERWORLD

Now do mind inter here our how precious gift more our parent home
traditional trysts tears, my renewed death offerings,
and keep here from your brother mulled many a tear he flawed to,
of their kin perpetual, brother, ever out here fare well.

—Louis Zukofsky *Catullus 101*

PROLOGUE

Viruses multiply at the beginning, tenacious classics,
with the bomb we forgot and the family sarcasm,
a picture labeled *squaw* and a miniature torah.
In the background, the conglomerate they repent
lives nearer than gerunds or future phobias.

To croak is a form of atonement on the first isthmus,
a quandary that can leave you lame in the movie
about Jesus, mumbling the word *troth*.

She demonstrates the abacus and performs Lenny
fortissimo. He doesn't have tertiary syphilis.
Ego has and hasn't arrived.

Emulate and imitate arrive together. A pair
in the parterre, a pander and a defector,

step from the desiccated pages of a red paperback.
Militants step from the pages of a newspaper.
Obstetricians toy with prolix addicts,
appalled by the idea of supernovas.

As a hot compress draws pus from a secret place
in the thigh of Virgo, events themselves briefly teach us.
This is not an invasion of what's amiss, no,
not a pacification of dreary logic, not an immolation
of the militantly mediocre. Imperfect prefects
lurk in the cynic's curser, young and loquacious,
forgetting the facile sector and conks' ether.
The teak veneer enters the cupidious quorum.

In vain, ignoramus. In vain, omniscience.
At first, Acheron doesn't strike a chord
as much as teriyaki or the sound of tenebrous.
The pyre consumes sermons and sarabands,
but they reappear in the inextricable tomes
of growing up indignant and sanguine,
divining what repulses the desired.

Once again, sepals wave before us,
but the pug never reaches the viscous aquifer,
the demesne of ramifications. Alas,
that's for the squeamish and magnanimous
after picky colloquies. With whom?
Ephebes? Please, return to praxis,
the evolution of a contradictory being.

Best to reread the paragraph about a numen.
Sin is immanent, right? A kyle for later?

Aberrant predictions explode some edifices,
co-opting quanta for the first time,
soon to be seminal in buskins. So irrelevant.
In the meantime, dairy worship fades,
magazines grant daily. Not pity, not pity,
but self-pity, that was understandable
over curry in front of the literal arras,
the feral expedients.

Profanity, renounced long ago, fills the vacuum
of reliquaries, a circle of nightmares
growing like stalagmites and persiflage.

It's time, albeit late, for that famous pair,
ingenuous and disingenuous, to discover
the sedulous abalone, the lubricious premium.

A sense of lack ends among Grandpa's acrostics,
the return of disgraced media, the divas
always missed through poor planning or whatnot.
Some bull about evisceration and tepidity.
Even spelunking. Meanwhile, nothing accrues
except newspaperese, which vies with velour
for Proserpina's gorgonzola.

Once again, a subliminal feeling of inadequacy
arises among bibulous souls on muggy shores,
always more of a world.

SIC FATUR LACRIMANS

(After the opening of Book VI of Virgil's *Aeneid*)

Sick fatter lack remains, classic admit it happiness
a tan deem you both is come are you mad bitter roar is.
A verdant peel a cup or us; tomb dented tenaciously
anchor a fund a bat navy set litter a curve I
pray taxing puppies. You mean him man us me catarrh dense
lettuce in his spear; cry it parsimony flame
abstruse in wane is seal kiss, party sapphires
check the rabbit selvage invent a quaff luminous monster.
Happiest a knee a sarcastic quibble salt a sap hollow
president horrendous I quip row cool secret a see be lie,
ant rum a mane, pet it, magnanimous coup I meant a minimum
deals inspire at vats apparent cleft a torah.
Yam abeyant trivia I look or sat quarrel attack.
  Dead all us, out famished, fudge ends man annoy reign
pry pet a bus pen necessary creed recoiled
in sway trumpeter jelly dozen of it at ark toes,

shall kid it cock well office tandem soup or ask it arch.
Read it us his premium terrace to be, foible, sock ravish
remit gum alarm pore it quay man attempt low.
In four of us let him androgynous; thumping repent us
key cropped us see (my serum!) septic quote onus
corporal nature; understand duck dessert a bus urn.
Contra a lot of them are irresponsible nose tell us:
hick crude elixir a mortar I suppose tock furtive
pacify mix them cogent us prolix by forms
minnow tourist I nest, venerable money maintain fan day,
hick labor ill dome us ate inextricable is error;
magnanimous renegade said enema miser tomorrow
dead all us if sedulous take time bog a squaw resolve it,
cake arrange fellow vestige. To cook marjoram
part them open intact, sinner it dollar, I care, harbors.
Bisque a knot us cause us a fin gerund hour row,
pisspot tree hike kidder a man us. Quinine protein insomnia
pearl edge rent coolers, knee yam premises a cot us
odd for it at quay one ephebe trivia I quiz actor does,
day phobic law key, fat turkey tally irregular:
"No oak is taxi by temper spectacular postscript;
none gray gay day intact oh septum act are you thank us
press it alright, toe tidy like taxes more by dentists."

Tail a bus add fat a knee (neck sacred more ranter
use a veering) to cross vacate all to intent please acre dose.
Excise move over let us engines rue pus in answer,
quality duking add to us scent him, us tea scent him,
one day ruined to tedium focus, response a civil lie.
Vent then errata lemon, come here go "pose carefully
Tempura" site; "day such days!" cooing tally a fan tee
ante for us sub atone vulture, no color on us,
nincompoop time answer coma; said pecked us in helm,
at rob affair cord a two men, Majorca over there eh
neck mortal assonance, add flautist new mine quandary
yam propeller day. "Case as in vote a procession,
troth" ate "a knee a? Case as? Neck when amount dehiscent
atone he time ignore ado must." Eddy leaf at a
count tick a wit. Gelid us too crisper during a concurrent
oats a tremor, fund it qua praxis wrecks peck tore abysmal:
"Feeble, grave is Troy I simper miser ate labor rest,
dare donate key paradise directly tell a manuscript
corpus in a yak he die, magnate abeyant terrace
tot marry a introduce tape and tusk are repast us
mass island gent is pretend aquifer are of:
I am tandem it alley eye forget aspirin moose hours.
Hack try on a tennis for it fortune a see coot a;

voice cuckoo purge a nay I am fastest park her agent,
deck a day hike qualms, quibble obstetrics ill yum tingles
glory a daredevil. Took a, O sanctimonious vat is,
price key adventures, day (known in debit a post cold
reign May is fat is) lasso consider a two crows
errant is a day or sag it attack a new minatory I.
Tum feeble ate trivia I solid ode murmur attempt plum
institute fuss Tosca tasty nominate he be.
Take woke we magnanimous rain is penetrate your nose is:
Hick ego name coat to assorted arcana calf at a
dictum eye again tip on ham, like toast exactly boy,
alma a, virus. Folly is tantrum neck harmony amend a,
nether battle availing rapid is lubricious vents;
it's a canister." Fine them date it ore look when die.
At fee be not dumb patience immanent in ant row
back at your fates, magnum see pecker oppose it
excuses a dame; tan tomato silly fatigue at
horseradish, fear a cord abdomens, finger it a premium.
Ask I am a dome us parterre ingenuous ken tomb
spontaneous vat is quaff errant response after hours:
"Oat and imagine is paid like a defunct a pear release
(said tear rye gravy or a man ant), in rag no lave in
dare dandy I veiny ant (mitt a honk defector occur),

said known it venison voluntary. Bell a, horrid a bell a,
ethyl rim mull to spume hunt then sanguine kernel.
Nonsense is to be necks and thus neck door attack astral
deferent; alley a sleigh show one part is a killer ease,
not us at hips idea; neck too crisp add it a you know
use qualm aberrant, come too supple sin ray bus against
was gent is it alum outcries no robbers herbs!
Cows are militant in conjunction a room horse spit a too crisp
external quite a room that lames.
Tuna quay demolish, said counter ardent or eat toe,
what to a take fortune ass synod. Via prime salutes
(quote minimal raises) gray a panderer a burb."
  Tail a bus exact it addict us coo may a sibilant
hoe rend us can it ambush us ant row quay removes it,
obscure is very involving: Hey affray no fur any
conclude it esteem you lose suspect or avert it apple low.
Hut premium kiss it furor ate rabid or a queer runt,
in keeping it a knee as heroes: "No null a labor room,
O Virgo, nova my face aches in open harbor surge it;
hominy pry cape he at quay animal make him anticipate rages.
No tomorrow: when doohickey ferny January gist
ticketer ate tenebrous appall us Acheron tea refuse us,
ear ad cons peck them carry genitor is at or a

counting god; do curiosity at acrostics a panda.
Ill them ego persiflage eight million sequences tell a
frippery his humor is mediocre exhaust a reception;
Ill a maim comity at a sitter marry a knee a make him
at any amiss pale logic mine a sky lick for a bat,
invalid us, fear is ultra sort him a necktie.
When, a taste supple experiment to a liminal dear one,
eat them oranges mandate debate. Gnat is patrician,
all maw, breaker, miser air a (protest numskull ambiance,
    necktie
next week I'm look is Hecate prefect it a furnace),
suppose it man is a cursor a conjugal or fey us
three keys a freight us kith are affordable wheat canneries,
see frat room poll exalt urn amortize redeem it
icky read it wavy am toe tens. Could these here, magnum
could member them all get in? Eat my jeans above someone."
  Tail a bus or a bat dick is orangutan about,
come sick or so loquacious: "Sat a sanguine a dive them,
throw and kiss the others, facile is the census aver no:
knock taste at quiddity pot it at tree on your did is;
said revoke are a grab them superadded evade or adore us,
hoe cope us, hick laborious. Pow key, quasi us move it
uppity out are dense effects it add ether a virtues,

disjoin it impotent. Tenant media omniscient vie,
Cocytus sinew lob ends circumvent it ant row.
Cutesy taunt us hammer mint tea, seat ants cupidious
big Stygian ignore like us, big snigger video
tartar a, ate insane or you're fat indulge air lab boring,
I keep a wiper paragon dapper us. Lattice arbor alpaca
hoary russet folly is it lent toe vim ignoramus,
union infer edicts soccer; hunk take it home is
loo cosset obscure is clawed unconventional umber.
Said no antedating tell his hope or too severe
or a coma squaw quiz disturb it are bore a fetus.
Hock see bee pull craw sue him ferry Proserpina moon us
and stick to it. Primeval also none defecate altar
hour yes, ate similar fronds skit virgin metal low.
Or go all to vestiges or you listen right report him
car pimento; numb quips avalanche fake elicits equator,
city fate evoking; alley turn on virile bus a list
vine carry nectar up odorous convey leery fellow.
Pry teriyaki examine them tea be corpus a mickey
(who nest kiss) totemic incest at funeral classes,
dumb consult a pet is no stroke in limb in appendix.
Set a bus hunk refer ante sue us ate con day sepulcher.
Duke knee grass pack all this; a prime apiary sun tow.

Sick deem him look us Styx is at rain envy vivid
aspic yes." Dick sit, precisely I'm new to it or a.
A knee is mice toad fix us luminous vulture
ingratitude linking ant rum, cacophony voluntary
event unanimous say come. Coos feed us a cot ace
it combs upper bus cure is vestige you figure.
Malt inter say savory sermon a saraband,
came soaking examine him vat is, quote core pus human dumb
dicker it. At quill he missing him in litter a sicko,
out vain era, vie dent indignant more tea peremptory,
missing him ale a den, quinine press down or alter
air a care a veer us mart them watch under it can't you.
Hectoring hick magnificent comas, hector ascertain
adlib though pug nose in sickness obey bat it hostler.
Post sawmill unfit victor spoil you have it a kill is,
dare don't know a knee I say say fortissimo heroes
add did a rat soak him, none inferior a executor.
Said to him, forty cavities person at a quorum conch,
demesne, and can't advocate in occur to me out of us,
emulate except a triton, see crater a dig numbest,
inter sacks a veering spew most immerse her at under.
Air go home nest make no care come clamor a frame about,
precipice pious a knee is. Timorous sea bee lye,

hold more a, fastidious flint ace a ram way sepulcher
conjure a more of us colloquy a duke or a certain.
It or in antique silver, stab ululate for arm;
pro can hunt picky I, son addicted secure a bus eyelids
fracas in the eye try base coon is it thistle robber
send it to her, absolving engine dismount a bus or not.
Neck not a knee as opera in tertiary prime
hoarder soaking pare a buskin a king it or arm us.
At quahog hip say sue a tryst icky cord evolutionary
aspect on sylvan immense, at sick fort a predator:
"Cynic see nobility how are we a saber a ram is
extend it namer intact now! When dome knee veer
who needs him data vat ace, me sin nay, look cutest."
Vixen fattest a rot, gem in I comfort a column buy
it's a sub or a very kyle of venery voluntary,
ate virid he sidereal solo. The maximal heroes
matter no sag knows it have this light us deprecator:
"East two kisses, oh, seek a feast, curse him quipper hours
derogate in lucre you be penguin divvy opacity
ram's humor. Took way, oh, dubious knit edifice ray bus,
diva parents." Sick effortless vestige oppress it
observance why significant, quoting during purges.
Pass scent silly taunt them prodder everlasting

quantum equipoise sent ocular serve are sequential.
Into you be venerate foul case grave violent aver knee,
tolling say clear us liquid yum way prairie elapse I
said a bus opt at is gem in a super arbor accede it,
discolor under a ripper almost aura repulse it.
Camisole it slivers broom olive rigor eviscerate
frond a veerer a nova, quote none sue a seminal tar boast,
at croak oaf head you tear it is circle dairy trunk hoes,
tall is alright species hourly front dentist or pack up
a lea, sick leaning crept about bratty events.
Curry pity needs us a stamp placid ask him to bring it
conk tantrum, and that is poor at subject a see belie.
  Neck minus in terror me seen them in literal too creed
fleabag incinerate ingrate of supreme affair about.
Principal pinging tidy is it robber a sector
ungentle structure a pyre am, cooing front ibis actress
in taxing latter at feral is ante compresses
constituting, decorating soup a refulgent a bizarre miss.
Par scalded us lattices attain an undaunting flames
expedient, corpus a way levant frigid is it unguent.
Fit gamuts. To remember to row deflate an opponent
purpureal cask super vest us, vellum in a note,
conic hunt. Parson gin disappear fare a true,

tryst administering, it subjects them more a parent them
averse eaten you wear a vacuum. Congestion cremate her
tour a donut, dapper, fuse so craters or live home.
Post qualm cone lapsing kin or us at flame a quiet it,
reliquary win it bibulous lover of fable lamb,
a sock weighs lexicons attack it corny niacin.
Eat them terse oak spoor a circle tool it under
bargains roar alleviate ramifications or leave eye,
lust for it quiver or stick it queen of isthmus verb a,
happiest a knee as in gent immolate sepal crumb
impound it sue a karma veer or remember to bomb way
mount a superior, queen unc me seen us abalone
take a tour I turn them quitting it persecute no man.
His act is proper an executor pry kept a sea belie.
Spelunking all too few it vast oak a man is hiatus,
scrupulous, toot a lack unique row them oar come here
tenebrous,
qualm superb you like powder ant impugn voluntary
tender it her pen is: tall easy say hail it is actress
false cabbage abundance soup a rod convex affair about.
Under lock come cry dicker run nominate I warn them.
What you wore hick premium knee grant yesterday you thank
us

constitutes front teak in very good vine a sock heard us,
and some of us carping media enter cornea cite as
ignore us opponent sack rice, the abominable prima,
folk evoke hands Hecate in colloquy air abacus potent them.
Supposing alien cultures tepid accrue roaring
recipient patter is. Hips a tree velour is sagging
a knee is motley you meant it to them magnify sorority
and suffer it, sterile them to be, Proserpina, vacuum;
some Stygian already nocturne as in cahoots arras
eat solid important tore roar them visceral flame is,
ping a supper roll yum funding ardent a bus ecstasy.
Account them pre me subliminal soul is it artist
so pet a bus muggy resolution and you go co-opted moo very
silver them, recycle canes ululate penumbras
adventitious day. "Pro cool, O pro cool is to, profane it,"
conglomerate vat is, "toe tow away abscess it allocate;
took away invade a via vagina where up affair them:
None can any of us opus, a knee a, none peck tore firm."
Tan tum is fat a furring ant row say him is it appear to;
ill adduce them hoed timid is voiding them pass a bus equity.
Die, quibbles imperial extant morrow, umbrella silent taste
eat Chaos eat Phlegethon, locomotive talk into it late,
sit me if us audit a low key, sit numen a vest row

panderer result a tear it call it immersion.

SIBILANCE

Sick and much fatter,
admit to all concerned
the time has come
to dent the tombs
with prayers for a puppy,
a luminous monster
who licks the president
whenever he's lying
about the minimum.

Follow your thin noses
from bisques to pisspots,
cooking and caring
with insomniac fervor
when we're gone.
It's OK to introduce
a couple of errors

into a column of numbers,
but any chicken fat
could upset the intent.

For now, ask questions,
even if the answers
strike you as errata
carefully composed
about the events on 33.
What a day! What a year!
Coo about that flautist
in Italia, simplicity
alongside the city's gravity:
keys and aspirin and rest.
Tusks and cuckoo clocks.
Qualms and tingles.

Patience alone won't help
with your fate again
in those rooms, those clothes.
Unreadable faces lash
the parterres, too,

with their nonsensical bells.
And the necks, the necks!
The necks sway on the quays
of the grayest burbs.

Follow the moving object
today, not tomorrow,
still the same January
Auntie refused us.
Next week, I'm visiting
the cannery with three keys.
Could we all get in?

Come exactly as you are—
sickly or loquacious,
ensnaring or ensnared.
Under the auspices
of the fixed census,
they're mingling ether,
mint tea and virtue,
but keep the paragon
by a sopping sign,

"No Antedating, Please."

If you're listening
to cities' leery fates,
examine mouths for mickeys,
the suck into a lair.
Repair the vulture's ear
with an old slogan,
"Out vain era, unfit victor,
you have your spoils."

Even around conches,
draw the line at tritons.
Don't clamor so much
about pious precipices
and boldfaced honeybees,
conjuring colloquies
and absolving engines.

Neither a sylvan aspect
nor a sick predator
appreciates the nobility.
Who needs his sword

and data and vats?
Matter has this light
we deprecate in observances
with everlasting prodding.
The discolored aura
even repulses novas.

In terror of pyres
and fleabags and actresses,
don't forget to row
the unguent to the tryst
in a perfect vacuum.
Lapsed kin douse
the flames themselves,
quivering for the queen
of the isthmus.

The executor's actions
are scrupulous, under glass.
Make sure to thank him
for what you wore,
the teak and wild rice,

and try to overlook

the abominable primas

and visceral inflammation.

Call it immersion.

THEY'RE THEIR THERE

I

Your eyes can't hide the scent
of the pear, bruised at the bottom
of the deep bowl of our hours.
The sun and its persistent ants
return to these parts tomorrow.
Bye-bye! Veins ferry our bodies
back uphill to the sole voice
no anger could ever thicken
with foam, to diminutive hands
poring over pages, weighing them.
This fare they're sharing,
outmoded wares from the back
of cool stalls, might lead you
to knit your steamy brow,
unworthy boarder, before eliciting

a response from littoral folk
about ragged oars and shrunken seas.
Red fowls head this way today,
but they won't lure a boar
to an uneven contest. In effect,
you're the only one who will.

II

I am this body, carefully packed,
sent with a pair of this
and that, our son and daughter,
our aunt who talks slowly
and buys hats that encourage me
to be vain and ascetic.
All those souls to get to know
during the sloppy pouring!
There's only one way to be fair
to their possessions today.
Cease nitpicking close to home
and wear a tie at the border.
The illicit, unlike the danger
of being too literal about needs,
rarely returns to haunt me.
From now on, leave the ore below.
To see is more than enough,

enough, not quite enough.

You've read about foul nights

in the lore, boors' daughters.

It affects your breathing.

III

Aye, we pare the horny skin
during the fifth rainbow of the day,
a day of storms and giddy breaks.
By pointing to the helper
in the enterprise, the poor child
who reproaches every century,
there won't ever become here,
free with a scarlet reflection
in icy water, free to bore
with rosy tales of yore.

AMONG SENSES

Our ties loosen
and change texture,

but the lies are good,
high in the grass

and in advance
of today's post.

The conjunction,
however, of a date

and ripening hips
and unseen tears,

an early effect
of many listings,

dampens the reception
of the pale watch.

A calf tenses.
You wince, too,

craving the rest
of those nights,

the dry premises
long since abandoned.

Then and there,
the base inspired

whole classes,
fading brands.

What bores!
What reports!

They can act

as well as act,

always hovering

among senses.

THE SEAL WORE OUT

Technically, the value drained away
when the image of the lion and lamb blurred.
No piece of paper in a trembling hand
patches up differences by the water anymore,
only appeals to tradition and force.

Droplets of water build up to the left
of the line, reminiscent of a healthy sweat,
but hardly telltale. The salty smell
lifts our spirits out of the frazzled state
that may be in our best interests today.

All those years, we spoke admiringly
of muscles and furs and indefatigability.
Now we walk up and down carping
until the keepers and repairmen appear
and the cycle begins all over again.

TENEBROUS CHILDREN

The bats and crones shouldn't be blamed for the dents
on the tombs, the smallest of which remain empty.
They swap tales about catarrhs and remissions,
false drawers yielding a fine crop of skeleton keys,
some hundreds of years old, others not yet born.
In the meantime, I'm dusting the earthenware urns
in the aisle of the bus, daydreaming about elixirs,
crude but very much to the point. A renegade?
Magnanimity, in such cases, rarely raises a fellow,
except vestigially. Like phobias. Like laws.
If only I had foreseen the cabby's impatience,
but there were so many oaks, and even more ants.
Instead of a daytrip to Majorca, a perfect postscript,
a day is reckoned as ruined. No tragedy, I guess,

nothing like the end of harmony in the neck,
receptions finally exhausted, only the thistles left.

So what if the icky tryst won't take place tomorrow
at the sick fort, where quahog shells and sabers
are strewn in a circle around vats of boiling numbers.
Who needs him anyway? Cold-blooded penguins
with a northeasterly style of French kissing,
insignificant observances and quotes during purgation?
And yet, as they say in Hartford, a silly scent
helps us creep past an argument about camisoles
and seminal dentists to the fringe of the event,
where tenebrous children rise to the indulgent air
of cloudy cataracts and transcontinental bargains
roaring in the distance. The rejection of spelunking
causes some to pause before an artificial cabbage.
Superb qualms are born every day, even on Sunday.

FIVE POEMS

I. *AVUNCULAR*

Well, the proper containment
seems to obtain among the islands,
even among gents. No hoary folly,
however much some of us carp.
Our often imperial quibbling,
little more than hypocrisy
and a final retreat from the idea
of daredevilry, tells much more
about impatience than foibles.
Read to them, air those cares,
no one knows glory's serial.
And stick with it. Advocating
no necessary race or religion,
the gist of January was waiting

and waiting to be kissed....
What? Exactly. Exactly, my boy.
Curry chicken, yes. Pity, no.
Anticipate the rages inside,
which tend to be most erosive,
and maybe even suffer them.
Sup tersely. Oaken, oaken.
Your spinster aunt, Aunt Annie—
Aunt Auntie to the kiddies—
stands with the annoyed mothers
on the day been is spelled bin,
every day and a long time ago.

II. *SKEPTICISM*

You mean that guy,
hooked on cynicism
and noble acts?
No. No grandson
deemed impractic
bruises his heel
on a jangling ring
of skeleton keys.

On that island,
right over there?
Dubious edifices
and educations,
a felitious ambiance
for telling noses.
That's the spelling.
A quipper's hour,
a zipper's hour.

Who needs the air
of miserly shadows?
Assorted arcana,
that's our learning,
weak as a teaser,
but a strong gambit
in an allegation.
It's strange but true.

III. *SOLACES*

Our sorority intact, fellow vestiges
Ghostly cooing fills the moist dark places
Petting works wonders on ruined days
Milestones in the loss of mutual esteem
Bite the tip off the baguette for her
The umbrellas, silent black mushrooms
Drifting through streets away from the river
They're cheap, everyone has one who wants one
A city destiny, even to leave the city
Already a nocturne by the streaked window
People want endings, smoking sadly forever
Lap up monologues couched in corners
Astral movies eventually repeat themselves
As long as we repeat ourselves
Come, come, who else will there ever be
These allergens and consanguinity
If you want to take up space and green
No one disagrees about the strain
Circling in an eddy for the time being

IV. *BITTER*

Yesterday, you thanked us,
and now there's no tomorrow.

Civil lies serve the usual suspects—
peace and quiet, the tragicomic hunt.

Tail the progeny of performers
and colorless plunderers

in the right place at a lax time,
an eternal formula....

If tombs are dented elsewhere
during a parsimonious tenancy,

the prima and abominable diva
promised to donate a key

to paradise, speedy and scented.
What more did you expect?

Sanctimony? Cautioning the aggrieved
to steer clear of loquacity?

Back with fate, perceived as the absence
of the orange aura around the mother,

everything is antedated to July,
personally discolored.

(The pier is being demolished,
the sleigh exhibited.)

Everyone hails the performers,
especially Pruneface and Flip,

until they sit down one evening
to a make-believe supper.

V. *WHIMSIES*

Those seals kissin' at 3, before almond bar, that was fun.
The flautist leaves out a part, the curiosity about acrostics
that ages one side of my neck during the principal pinging.
The ticketer stays out front, polishing the luminous bird,
while a moose plays in the dark above us, under lock and key,
the walls of her cask so purple, so velvety, so enveloping.
Muggy resolutions issuing from the palace on the isthmus
don't add up on the abacas. You know what? You-know-
  who
sorts the ties of one of the great-grandsons, glimpsing
tidy toes through a half-open door, the overall harmony
of the naturally selected muscle and bone structures.
Another bilious lover of fables, a protected species now,
defects to the astral contingent on a foggy sylvan morning.
Convey our invitation to the leery, weavers of critiques
and colloquia from the less-muddy principalities to the west,

descendants of the ancient folk, singing in the open air.

After all, we already have thistle robbers near our apiaries.

Buses' tailed. Sacks of dried leaves interred in urns.

Classes chanting slogans. So challenging, so much fun!

Once I forgot to row. They reeled in the diamonds anyway,

wise not to fear a shaggy piton in an underwater range.

The tides don't get that low in the Old World. Not yet.

CAPE

An envelope lies above the watermark
Cured by alternation

Inside, hearts are ground
To grains of stone, our manifold

So many whites at the end of times
Tans among the whites, calculated figures
One was too rough on the wrong day
One was too rough on the right day
I was bruised by the reduction

Water

She puts a stop, wrapping the sandy cape around her
Not the coolness, but the brightness below the top
Fireweed beyond the soft tar, a sick porcupine

A mirage wavers at the vanishing point

We reach it momentarily or never

Come, come, think of the row

Halfway around the world, "Cantico di Frate Sole"

The same tone coaxed out of its embalming velvet and orreries

The white spit

Lies in front of us

Waves

Santa Monica

Scary lists

A revolution

All the irritations of a dive

Did he say what I think

If he said what you think

Watch the pool shark

He takes the cue

The surface plays tricks
Not smooth, not smooth, as a courtesy to light
I thought for a minute, Jesus
In her lap and other low places
Tiny in the scheme, but reminders
Rage and illusions afterward, glassiness
How they're contained by the body

Her last stroke left me high and dry
So complete
Incomplete

Palms burn

I heard what befell the seal
In blinding fields of sugars
The date was sweet

DUSTING THE URNS

I was dusting the urns in the aisle of the bus
the day agoraphobia and triskaidekaphobia
were outlawed, and pyrophobia enshrined.
The tans were bitter in the batty Navy.
As lettuce caught fire, the abstruse party
invented other monsters for secret president,
principal beneficiary of a magnanimous coup.
Cf. "Abeyant Trivia" or "The Altruists."
The reign of fudge and trumpeter jelly
alarmed gums to androgynous repentance,
recommended serums. As for those urns,
furtive tocks nested venerably among them
in irresponsible prolixity, noisy cogency,
each and every fan day in the hiccup dome.
Tomorrow's enema thwarted sedulous resolutions.
The sinister, intact by and large, contributed
to protein insomnia in both of us. Her cot.
Your pearl coolers. Her pearl coolers.

Spectacular taxis converged on the gray act,
charging an acre a dose, pus in response.
High-quality duking scented him out
in the lemon vent. Our helm was pecked.
Mortal assonance, aborted masochism—
a quandary about mines propelled daytime
to a concurrent wit. Manuscripts showed
misers eating on an abeyant terrace
among taped tusks and moose aspirin.
Tennis fortunes led to the cuckoo purge.
Obstetric quibbles, truly post-cold,
reigned in May among attempted murmurs
to consider crows, instituting a big fuss.
Magnanimous rain on nether battlefields,
immanent patience, dated the ore forever.
You silly tomato, tear gravy concealed
the errant response of the veiny defector,
whose voluntary bell survived the astral attack
in a deferent alley among supple outcries.
Cows were militant, prime candidates to salute
with sibilant coos involving fur. Yes.
I lost the suspect at the premium hut,
knees the true heroes here, face aches.

’Twas a ferny January around the counting god,
curious about acrostics’ eight million sequences.
The sitter married a sky lick, purest product
of a liminal experiment to mandate oranges
in a numbskull ambience, a perfect furnace.
The room poll came back in wavy tens
from the sanguine dive, sans orangutan bites.
The laborious key, planted by a tree, belonged
to an omniscient media tenant with a cockeyed lob.
His cutesy hammer almost hobbled the air lab,
all $100 million, messing up the moon ferry.
A similar skit executed in virgin metal
touched off a car avalanche at the fake equator,
turned virile, nectar from a blank to be filled
in funeral classes. The Duke’s appendix
envied the rain. The sun’s secret tow
linked the cot ace with ingratitude,
and so we returned to the bus, to cures
instead of quote-unquote cores, missing litters
in the peremptory tea, missing dens
in the care mart, magnificent comas
for all post-sawmill cavities people.
The numbest crater clamored for a frame,

the picky flint. The Duke's latest colloquy
secured the eyelids from the try base
in its tertiary prime as buskin hoarder
and extended namer. At the comfort column,
voluntary subs feasted on knit edifices,
everlasting prodders to the liquid yum.
Broom slivers repulsed auras as well as tar boasts,
circling species on the hourly front
with a placid stamp. That subjected a sea
of principal pinging and super supers
to the expedient unguents. Fares disappeared
in the leather vest with the donut fuse,
then flamed in quiet, terse but corny spoor.

VERBA SANCTA

The court deems I dented her anchor
Reminders tax the county salting to annoy us
Yes she recoiled when I kidded by cocking the toy
I arched backward upon academic remittance
Funny thumping delays crop up during pacification
We nest and part the waters to hike
Teachers quiz the ability to tidy and neck
So the man excises ancient ruing no one vents in any event
The baby's cooing pecked the eddy where the arm counts
Concoctions purging guests parked helter-skelter
The deck sags the roof of her murmur and our fuss
Penetrating tips the amends back to availing
To excuse fingers the decision to release
Skis lane the spring to demolish and counter
The yes man salutes whoever tails pathetic addicts
As long as the weaker rends to ambush and thus affray the
    pilfered
The distant esteems to avert the aching for intimacy

Of busybodies prying by anticipating the quote that truly
appalls
All marry to lick and later experiment by mandating
The silly exalt the few who redeem and amortize
Always as he avers the knock revokes and evades anger
She copes with lobs to circumvent the hammering
It's possible to infer a claw the blast disturbs
Sue the prick/cunt for defecating on the capacity to report
I faked the afternoon to turn on a light and examine
The way the leaders consult by referring
Con, con, con, tow until they stick
To comb is to dither today, altering the direction
They ad-lib in order to obey without emulating
If anyone immerses herself, she spews and clamors
Until they ram the cart, occasioning a stab at ululation
Or some such means to secure and base the precise soaking
By arming the mesmerized, comforting everyone who sags in
peace
He derogates the similar to divvy the refund
Their verbiage oppresses more than taunting as a means to
venerate
Regulation elapsing before I accede to slivering
It figuratively eviscerates their boasts and croaks, hoeing the

unneeded
She packs up everything that crept along and was eventually
stamped
For incineration, decoration, souping up
If we miss scalding, it's still possible to attain a perfect
deflation
Vest the pension to administer prolonged subjection
To parenting, which teaches the fusion of tools
It alleviates to lust and even quiver to impound assets
Quitting lets you toot and impugn
They tender the hail to constitute a condition
He cites what I should ignore to sack and accrue
Magnifying mooing in order to profane
The body that allocates the rips to areas of heaviest furring
Then they adduce the audit as evidence of immersion

POLYMORPHOUS PERVERSITY

It's painful to admit whoever came, mad to have been grazed by a bat, set up and ready for spears rising from the litter of little and big days, days all the same, they cried. The seal wore out at the end. One end was left when the cock awakened. Well, the arch gave no thought to the sock until the right key. You have to admire the crop, by nature almost a lot, an unlikely fellow to advance the cause for a hike. The edge crosses the qualities of the dukes to the mettle, civil in the extreme. Pose for a pack before the affair leads me to the mine. Must? To wit, we know rags. The sitter didn't budge from her post near the window. Licks. With this pot, to cope tells. I convey my frame to the rest of the bee. Take a stab at the concrete and abstract matter, rough and amorphous. Tolls take a toll, for sure, in front of the front. The true stamp of a subject wears. On the mount, the forgotten structure hails the run, but the culture in the lab prizes the firm.

ANTISTROPHES

The belts tighten
and stay the same color,

but the truth is no good,
buried in concrete

somewhere in the rear
of yesterday's beam.

The disjunction,
moreover, of solitude

and thinning petals
and visible joy,

a late cause
of few irons,

heightens the rejection
of the ruddy vacuum.

Every calf relaxes.
They yawn, alone,

tired of the exhaustion
of this daylight,

the slippery conclusions
lately embraced.

Here and now,
the lofty deflates

a select few,
brightening generics.

What raconteurs!
What one-liners!

We can’t pass

as well as pass,

never grounded

in the senseless.

AFTER THE TIME OF SHARED REFERENCES

That dinner at the Hotel on the Cay
stands out for the depthlessness
of a boy's jealousy of his little sister.
The adults rowed back in silence.
Forget the meeting at the tee,
even without any kids in tow.

Years later, the throbbing toe returns
as he drinks tea with Dally
and Margarita prepares the roe.
Far away, the Ayatollah snickers
at the famous cake in the shape of a key.

A RETROSPECTIVE GLANCE

Did the vats inspire
the little men to dream

and the metallic women to care
about intact harbors,

refusing to acknowledge
a you-know-what?

That repulsed the kids
more than any freight of keys

hidden for all to see
in a dubiously knit edifice,

mercifully overlooked
in the talk about locomotion.

THE SKELETON AS A WORK OF ART

are you mad

a verdant peel   dented tombs

you mean him

parsimonious flames

seals kiss   party sapphires

luminous monster

a sarcastic quibble

pet it   magnanimous coup

inspire at vats

dead all us   fudge ends

necessary creed

trumpeter jelly

office tandem

read his foibles to us

remit the gum

androgynous thumping

cropped key septic quote

a bus urn

nose tells us

crude elixir

maintain fan day

inextricable is error

magnanimous renegade miserly tomorrow

fellow vestige

intact harbors

phobic law irregular tally

no oak is a taxi spectacular postscript

none gray

tidy toe

let us engines answer

one day ruined civil lie

.

pecked our helm

Majorca over there, eh

add flautists

eddy leaf

count ticks among wits

concurrent oats

donate a key to paradise

island gent

forget aspirin moose hours

purge a nay park her agent

hike qualms

glory's a daredevil sanctimonious vat

murmuring an ode

institute a fuss

penetrate your nose

assorted arcana

exactly, boy

folly is a tantrum   neck harmony

nether battle

it's a canister

not dumb patience

back at your fates

fear a cord   finger it

response after hours

pear release

sanguine kernel

astral attack

sleigh show

a you-know-what

come too supple

demolished quay

minimal raises

tail a bus

obscure is very involving

esteem you lose

premium hut

anticipate rages

no tomorrow January gist

the ticketer ate

curiosity about acrostics

eight million sequences

exhaust a reception

sort his neckties

miser air   protest numskull ambiance

a freight of keys

eat my jeans

come so loquacious

cutesy taunt

indulge air

hoary folly

take it home

no antedating

and stick to it

listen right   report him

evoking a city fate

convey the leery fellow

funeral classes

pack all this   a prime apiary

deem him sick   vivid envy

voluntary cacophony

coos feed

out vain era peremptory tea

air a care
hectoring hick

post sawmill

none inferior

and can’t advocate
emulate except for his triton
inter the sacks

fastidious flint
conjure a duke for a colloquy

addicted son
thistle robber
dismount a bus

icky cord

sick fort

cynics see nobility

intact now

who needs him

a very kyle of venery

sidereal solo

seek a feast a quipper's hour

divvy opacity

dubious knit edifice

the diva's parents effortless vestige

quoting during purges

clear us

almost aura

bratty events

curry pity

and that is a poor subject

incinerate the fleabag

principal pinging

cooing front

undaunting flames

fit gamuts   to remember to row

purpureal cask

conic hunt

administering a tryst   subjects them

live at home

bibulous lover of fables

weighs lexicons

terse oak

bargains roar   alleviate ramifications

lust for it   queen of the isthmus

sepal crumbs

his act is proper
all too few spelunking
come here tenebrous
superb qualm
hail it's the actress
false cabbage
under lock
what you wore yesterday you
thanked us
very good vine
and some of us carping
abominable prima
evokes hands

recipient patter
you meant it to them
and suffer it
already a nocturne
visceral flame

muggy resolution   and you go co-opted

adventitious day

not any of us can

a furring

imperial quibbles   silent umbrellas

locomotive talk

low-key audits

call it immersion

EPILOGUE

Nowadays, the bodies in the ferry look more diminutive than
ever.
Unworthy in the seas of this contest. Vain and ascetic.
The pouring at the border, dangerously literal,
slows their breathing to speed the growth of horn.

Scarlet ice melts all over a dress, tisk-tisk, tisk-tisk,
marring the print of tombs and skeleton keys and earthenware
urns.
But let me assure you, the bus won't stop for a concluding
unscientific postscript,
not after receptions at a fort where vats boil under
microscopes.

The best quotes come from doctors and rhetoricians.
"Cataracts or catachresis, with which should we begin?"
On a transcontinental day, when animal images blur
on trembling paper, traditions and furs lie high in the grass.

But they're fading, I'm afraid, like the black poodle puppy
the president fed lobster bisque in his insomnia.
Such errors are the unlikely keys to rest,
the qualms and tingling that briefly postpone fate.

The rooms survive in an unreadable book.
With the quays. With Auntie. Ensnared "by a member of the
    opposite sex."
The Czar's census taker improves the name of the paragon,
not exactly a victor climbing out of a precipice....

The engine needs more data, to its everlasting credit.
We find discoloration someplace on each actress.
No perfect vacuum. If we're scrupulous,
hypocrisy will retreat to the oaken dining rooms.

Aunt Auntie will take care of everything, even the spelling.
She isn't married to our arcane sorority,
identity of last resort, the loss of self-esteem.
The bite before the silence for anyone who wants it.

But the astral plane recedes. We don't have enough fog, it
    turns out.
Allergens encircle our progeny. And plunderers.
This is not the right place in the eternal formula
(too close to sanctimony and fateful antedating).

Pruneface didn't linger on the pier near the Renaissance
    prison.
Salted almonds beat curiosity any day, he said,
but what comes last, acrostics or natural selection?
What should be protected after Thrones, Principalities,
    Powers?

Somehow, thistle didn't wash up in the Old World.
The cure sank in the soft tar, next to an inexplicable porcupine,
embalmed by God or Nature or Ralph Waldo Emerson.
The chemical composition of spit still lay in front of us.

What are they? So tiny, so nearly hidden in the body politic,
so incomplete. Perhaps the blinding fields
and unnecessary navies will give birth to altruists,
but for now, proteins and taxi rides preoccupy insomniacs.

The vents are carved from fresh lemons. Aspirin sugar.
Defectors follow this vein to the voluntary bell, a survivor
of resplendent knees, sky-sitting at the fake equator,
where omniscient media cover funeral classes.

At the most out-of-the-way mart, their comforts greet us.
The supers of endless wings, with unmentionable fare,
a matter for the county that condemned releases.
The experiment didn't work, but it should be emulated.

Carts still soak to a purpose somewhere, if not here,
just as refunds haven't arrived to be venerated
and incineration retains its earlier meanings.
Deflation and immersion are painful to admit, aren't they?

What would that day be like? Would we be civil
near the window, when solitude's so much more desirable?
When thinning takes hold and vision loses hold
in either case? This isn't a vacuum, yawning alone.

This is how it is with conclusions: rarely uplifting,

with fewer lovers in the wing, no sailor's snug harbor so far.
The you-know-what forsakes the tenacious for the credible.
Phobias are outlawed, but atonement is here to stay.

No one steps lively from the secret place in the cursor,
repulsing the desired. But once this evolution
reaches a kyle of venery, co-opting for the last time,
persiflage will reign with Proserpina.

About THE EDGE OF THE UNDERWORLD:

After studying Louis Zukofsky's Rudens *in graduate school, I always wanted to write a homophonic translation. A decade later, I settled on the long opening of Book VI of Virgil's* Aeneid*, the famous Underworld book, and wrote "Sic Fatur Lacrimans." Soon afterward, sensing the translation itself needed translation, I decided to derive other poems from the words and phrases of "Sic Fatur Lacrimans"—poems that would be connected to the long poem and to each other, in a sort of literary Rayonism. I saw the book as the verbal equivalent of St. Sebastian pierced by arrows, with "Sic Fatur Lacrimans" as St. Sebastian and the shorter poems as the arrows, crisscrossing each other.*

Michael Handler Ruby is the author of four other books of poetry—**At an Intersection** (Alef Books, 2002), **Window on the City** (BlazeVOX [books], 2006), **Fleeting Memories** (Ugly Duckling Presse ebook, 2008) and **Compulsive Words** (BlazeVOX, 2010)—and the editor of **Washtenaw County Jail and Other Writings** by David Herfort (Xlibris, 2005). A graduate of Harvard College and Brown University's writing program, he lives in Brooklyn and works as an editor at *The Wall Street Journal.*

5104999R0

Made in the USA
Charleston, SC
30 April 2010